WILD ANIMALS

ANACONDAS

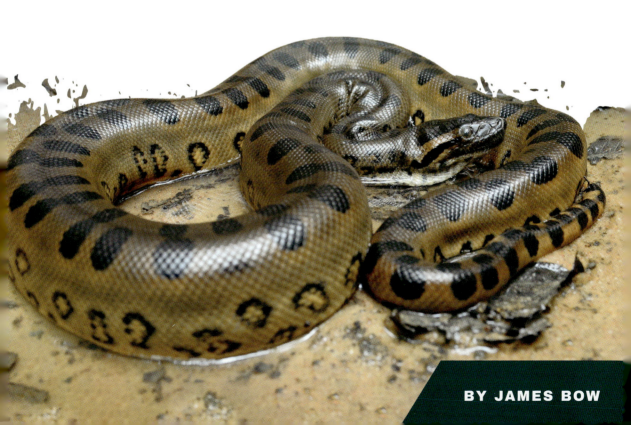

BY JAMES BOW

WWW.APEXEDITIONS.COM

Copyright © 2023 by Apex Editions, Mendota Heights, MN 55120. All rights reserved. No part of this book may be reproduced or utilized in any form or by any means without written permission from the publisher.

Apex is distributed by North Star Editions:
sales@northstareditions.com | 888-417-0195

Produced for Apex by Red Line Editorial.

Photographs ©: iStockphoto, cover, 6, 10–11, 14; Shutterstock Images, 1, 4–5, 7, 12–13, 15, 16–17, 18, 20, 21, 22–23, 24–25, 26–27, 29; Francois Gohier/Science Source, 8–9

Library of Congress Control Number: 2022910533

ISBN
978-1-63738-440-4 (hardcover)
978-1-63738-467-1 (paperback)
978-1-63738-518-0 (ebook pdf)
978-1-63738-494-7 (hosted ebook)

Printed in the United States of America
Mankato, MN
012023

NOTE TO PARENTS AND EDUCATORS

Apex books are designed to build literacy skills in striving readers. Exciting, high-interest content attracts and holds readers' attention. The text is carefully leveled to allow students to achieve success quickly. Additional features, such as bolded glossary words for difficult terms, help build comprehension.

CHAPTER 1
A TIGHT SQUEEZE 4

CHAPTER 2
STRONG SNAKES 10

CHAPTER 3
CATCHING PREY 16

CHAPTER 4
LIFE IN THE WILD 22

COMPREHENSION QUESTIONS • 28
GLOSSARY • 30
TO LEARN MORE • 31
ABOUT THE AUTHOR • 31
INDEX • 32

CHAPTER 1

A TIGHT SQUEEZE

An anaconda swims slowly. Only its head shows above the water. It sees a deer walk toward the river.

Anacondas are excellent swimmers.

The anaconda surges forward and strikes. Its jaws clamp onto the deer's neck. The snake wraps its body around the deer. Then it squeezes until the deer stops moving.

Anacondas have several rows of sharp teeth.

Anacondas curl their bodies to squeeze tightly.

A STRONG BITE

Anacondas have sharp teeth. They can kill small prey by biting. The teeth help anacondas grip large prey, too. They curve backward and pull the prey into the snakes' mouths.

The anaconda opens its jaws wide. It swallows the deer in one big bite. Then it rests. It won't need to eat again for months.

A snake's body shows a bulge after eating something big.

FAST FACT
An anaconda's flexible jaws can stretch three times as wide as its head.

CHAPTER 2

STRONG SNAKES

Anacondas are huge snakes. They can grow 30 feet (9 m) long. And they can weigh 550 pounds (249 kg).

An anaconda's long body has many strong muscles.

There are four **species** of anacondas. Green anacondas are the biggest. The Beni, black-spotted anaconda, and yellow anaconda are smaller.

FAST FACT

Anacondas can have yellow, green, or brown scales.

Anacondas' colorings help them blend in and hide.

Green anacondas mainly live in Colombia, Brazil, and Venezuela.

Anacondas are **native** to South America. Many live in **tropical** rain forests. Anacondas spend most of their time in slow-moving water. They are often found in swamps and rivers.

FAR FROM HOME

Some anacondas live far away from South America. For example, some live in the Florida Everglades. The snakes were probably brought there as pets. Then they escaped.

The Everglades is a large, marshy area that is home to many animals.

CHAPTER 3

CATCHING PREY

Anacondas are **carnivores**. They eat many animals, including deer, turtles, and wild pigs. The snakes often hide and wait for prey.

Anacondas sometimes catch and eat large birds.

Anacondas don't hear very well. So, they rely on their sense of smell. They can also sense body heat and **vibrations** from nearby animals.

FAST FACT
Anacondas flick their tongues to smell. They pick up scents in the air.

◀ **Like many snakes, anacondas have forked tongues.**

Anacondas coil their bodies in loops around their prey.

When an animal gets close, an anaconda attacks. It squeezes its prey until the prey can't breathe. Then it swallows the prey whole.

REST TO DIGEST

Anacondas often eat huge amounts of food at once. This food can take days to digest. Sometimes anacondas can't move during this time. So, they find safe places to rest.

Anacondas only need to hunt every few weeks.

CHAPTER 4

LIFE IN THE WILD

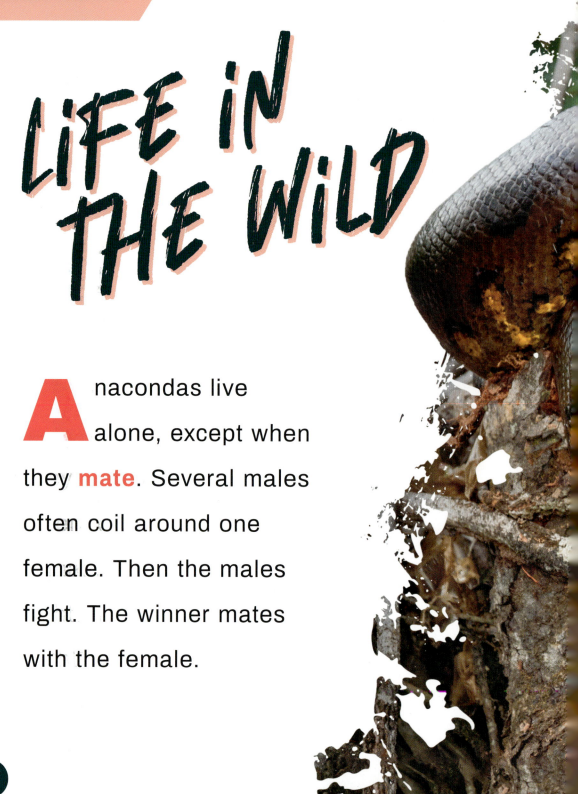

Anacondas live alone, except when they **mate**. Several males often coil around one female. Then the males fight. The winner mates with the female.

Female anacondas are much bigger than males.

After mating, female anacondas give birth to live babies. One female may have 20 to 40 babies at a time. The young snakes live on their own right away.

WATCH OUT!

Female anacondas sometimes eat males after they mate. That gives the females extra energy. After that, females might not eat until their babies are born.

Unlike many snakes, anacondas do not lay eggs.

FAST FACT

Anacondas live about 10 years in the wild.

At first, baby anacondas are just 2 feet (0.6 m) long. But they grow fast. After three to four years, they become adults. And they never stop growing.

Baby anacondas can hunt right after they are born.

COMPREHENSION
QUESTIONS

Write your answers on a separate piece of paper.

1. Write a sentence describing what anacondas eat.

2. Anacondas spend most of their time in the water. Do you enjoy swimming? Why or why not?

3. Where do most anacondas live?

- **A.** North America
- **B.** South America
- **C.** Florida

4. How do anacondas usually kill large prey?

- **A.** They drag the animal into the water.
- **B.** They squeeze until the animal dies.
- **C.** They bite once and leave the animal.

5. What does **strikes** mean in this book?

The anaconda surges forward and strikes. Its jaws clamp onto the deer's neck.

    A. bites quickly
    B. hides underwater
    C. stays still

6. What does **scents** mean in this book?

Anacondas flick their tongues to smell. They pick up scents in the air.

    A. tastes
    B. smells
    C. perfumes

Answer key on page 32.

GLOSSARY

carnivores
Animals that eat meat.

digest
To break down so the body can get energy from it.

mate
To form a pair and come together to have babies.

native
Originally living in an area.

prey
Animals that are hunted and eaten by other animals.

species
Groups of animals or plants that are similar and can breed with one another.

tropical
Having weather that is often warm and wet.

vibrations
Tiny back-and-forth movements.

BOOKS

Adamson, Thomas K. *Anaconda vs. Jaguar*. Minneapolis: Bellwether Media, 2020.

Hamilton, S. L. *Anacondas*. Minneapolis: Abdo Publishing, 2019.

Jaycox, Jaclyn. *Anacondas*. North Mankato, MN: Capstone Press, 2020.

ONLINE RESOURCES

Visit **www.apexeditions.com** to find links and resources related to this title.

ABOUT THE AUTHOR

James Bow writes novels and nonfiction children's books. He loves wild animals but knows to give them lots of space.

INDEX

B
babies, 24–25, 27
Beni, 12
bite, 7–8
black-spotted anaconda, 12

D
digest, 21

E
Everglades, 15

G
green anaconda, 12

J
jaws, 6, 8–9

M
mating, 22, 24–25

P
prey, 7, 16, 20

R
rain forests, 14
rivers, 4, 14

S
scales, 12
sense, 19
South America, 14–15
species, 12
squeeze, 6, 20
swamps, 14

T
teeth, 7

Y
yellow anaconda, 12

ANSWER KEY:
1. Answers will vary; 2. Answers will vary; 3. B; 4. B; 5. A; 6. B